# Bizarre CHRISTMAS Bible Stories

The **Kingmakers,**
The **Priest's Underwear,**
and **3** other
**CHRISTMAS STORIES**

BY **Dan Cooley**
POEMS BY **Janice Cooley Jones**

# ACCLAIM

"Simply put, author Dan Cooley's Bizarre Bible Stories and Bizarre Bible Stories 2! utilize a vernacular, contemporary writing style intended to reach an audience of children and youth with solid Christian doctrine and practical application. The discussion questions interspersed throughout the text are thoughtfully designed to promote interaction between parents and their children on numerous topics of interest. Cooley's books reflect his passion for providing spiritual food to children in a manner they can easily digest. His attention to detail is evident from cover to cover."
- **DR. GENE A. GETZ**
    Author of over 50 books including
    *The Measure of a Man*,
    President of the Center for Church Renewal

"Paul urged Timothy: 'you know those from whom you learned...' These captivating biographies and stories will equip and encourage parents, youth pastors and others who want to ensure the enduring faith of youth in the church."
- **DARYL BUSBY, PHD**
    Dean of Canadian Baptist Seminary,
    Director of DMN Program,
    ACTS Seminaries, TWU

# ACCLAIM

"Finally, a book that illuminates some of the coolest, oddest, and fantastical true stories of the Bible that, when read, young people can say, 'Wow! God really wants me to be THAT radical? THAT powerful? THAT bold?' Dan Cooley does this in the simplest and most profound way…he inspires students to read the stories in the Bible for themselves. Study it. Glean from it. And then go into the real world and live it.
 – **CHAD BARRETT**
  Author of *Journey to Freedom: The Pursuit of Authentic Fellowship Among Men,*
  Director of Child Evangelism Fellowship,
  Houston, Texas

"WOW! As a mother of two boys, I certainly see the need to ground our children spiritually. Dan's book is a tool to help us as parents ground our children in the Word. Dan pulls you into the Scripture and gives you a glimpse of what it was like. He encourages you to dig in God's Word and pull out God's personal message to you. There is no greater blessing than bringing God's Word to life for our children!"
 – **SUSAN WEAGANT**
  Author of *Essentials of the Heart*

All rights reserved. No part of this publication may be reproduced, stored in a retrieval system, or transmitted in any form or by any means — for example, electronic, photocopy, recording — without the prior written permission of the publisher. The only exception is brief quotations in printed reviews. Library of Congress Cataloging-in-Publication Data

Unless otherwise indicated, Scripture is taken from the Holy Bible, New Living Translation, copyright © 1996. Used by permission of Tyndale House Publishers, Inc., Wheaton, IL 60189. All rights reserved.

Scripture marked GOD'S WORD is taken from GOD'S WORD and used by permission. Copyright 1995 by God's Word to the Nations Bible Society. All rights reserved.

Scripture marked ICB is taken from the International Children's Bible, New Century Version, copyright © 1983, 1986, 1988 by Word Publishing, Dallas, TX 75039. Used by permission.

Scripture marked NIV or NIV2011 is taken from the HOLY BIBLE, NEW INTERNATIONAL VERSION®. NIV®. Copyright © 1973, 1978, 1984, 2011 by International Bible Society. Used by permission of Zondervan. All rights reserved.

Scripture marked MESSAGE is taken from THE MESSAGE. Copyright © by Eugene H. Peterson 1993, 1994, 1995. Used by permission of NavPress Publishing Group.

# Contents

**STORY 1**
The Priest's Underwear ........................................... 1
Scripture Passage: Luke 2:8-18

**STORY 2:**
Don't Name Your Dog Legion ................................. 15
Scripture Passage: Philippians 2:6-11

**STORY 3**:
Don't Mess with Harry ............................................ 29
The Passage: John 1:1-14

**STORY 4**
The Kingmakers ...................................................... 43
The Passage: Matthew 2:1-12

**STORY 5:**
Strange Sam ........................................................... 58
The Passage: Matthew 2:1-2

## STORY 1:

# The Priest's Underwear

**Scripture Passage:** Luke 2:8–18

**If God told you He was going to meet you for lunch tomorrow, how would you prepare?**

**What would you wear?**

Let's jump in a time machine, and listen in on a shepherd's conversation from 2000 years ago. Oliver was a shepherd's apprentice, and Emerson was his big brother. They should have been asleep, but the ground seemed harder and the air colder on this night, so they were sitting up talking. Oliver was playing with a beetle, flipping it upside-down and watching it struggle to get back on its feet. Emerson was concerned for the beetle, for good reason.

**THEN EMERSON SAID...**

# "Hey Oliver, why don't

you let that beetle go? You won't be a shepherd's apprentice much longer. You'll be working alone soon. Do you like shepherding any better now?"

Oliver scooted his bottom over to a flatter rock and decided to shoot straight with his big brother. "Honestly Emerson, I still hate this job. Roman warhorses are cool. Even cats catch mice. But sheep? They get lost, eat themselves sick, and are dumb enough to follow each other off a cliff. Besides that, sheep poop stinks, the pay is lousy, we sleep on rocks, and people make fun of us. This job sucks."

"Well, about those sheep," Emerson admitted. "I just always figured it was job security, them being too dumb and stubborn to make it on their own. They need a shepherd to love them in spite of their dirt. Then they are okay."

"No, then they still stink."

Emerson heard a sound. Maybe nothing, maybe wolves. He threw some logs on the fire for safety. Emerson wanted his brother to enjoy being a shepherd like he and their father did. So he asked, "You do know this is one of the most important jobs in history — right? You do know what Abraham's job was — from the book of Genesis?"

"A shepherd."

"Right. And Moses. What made him so great? It wasn't growing up as some rich Egyptian prince. Nope, it took forty years of shepherding to make a man out of him. And who was the greatest King who ever lived?"

Oliver, moving out of the smoke said, "Well, Solomon was the wisest, but I like David best."

"Right, and what was David's first job? A shepherd. We were rich, rugged and important."

Oliver looked down at the struggling beetle. He knew he shouldn't, but he put it in the edge of the fire where it would glow red and pop in a couple minutes. He never seemed ready for the Pop! which made it fun. Then he responded, "I already know those stories — but being a shepherd isn't cool anymore. It's been 1000 years since David was king. Now someone else owns the sheep, and we're stuck out here homeless, sleeping on rocks, with no chance for an education or a future, waiting for a beetle to pop. What's so great about that?"

Emerson was quiet. Rich people in Jerusalem did own the sheep — the shepherds just managed them for the owners. "Okay, you're right," he said, "but we really aren't homeless. We have the tower of Eder to take refuge in, when weather gets bad. We wrap up the new lambs in swaddling clothes to make sure they stay spotless for Temple sacrifices, and then lay them in the mangers until they calm down."

POP!

"Poor beetle. I wish you'd quit doing that. I'll admit, our language is rough, but at least we say what we mean. Just because we get convicted for every theft in town doesn't mean we're guilty of 'em. If they paid us what we were worth, we wouldn't have to steal so much! Anyway, I like paying no taxes…"

Oliver stuffed his dirty hands in his empty pockets, "That's because we have no money to pay taxes with!"

"OK, at least we don't have to go to church."

Oliver found another beetle. His lucky night. He saved it for later and thought about not going to church. He wasn't so happy about that. He was embarrassed, but he looked Emerson in the eyes anyway and said, "We don't go to church because they wouldn't let us in the Temple if we begged to get in. What's so great about that? Don't laugh at me, but I'd like to go to the Temple. Just once, I'd like to see what the Temple looks like on the inside — to smell the incense and hear the music and worship with everyone else. You remember when we took the lambs to Passover last spring, don't you? That priest was such a jerk. All we asked was to go into the Temple outer courts after selling him the lambs.

'Oh no, I couldn't let you do that,' he sneered, 'you shepherds are unclean. I can't let your kind into the Temple yard. You can't come into the presence of God!' I'll never forget him telling us that."

"Right," Emerson said, "but do you remember what I did then? 'You're dirty too!' I shouted, and slapped him in the face. He couldn't enter the temple for Passover either because he was touched by an 'unclean shepherd.' Pompous idiot. It served him right."

"Yeah, the look on his face was great! But, I'd still like to worship —"

"Well, maybe we're not good enough to come to God. But when we're out here, under the stars, it seems as if God has already come to us. Maybe we're as close to God out here as we would be at the Temple. Besides, have you forgotten what happened last year? We were camping by the Tower of Eder, by Bethlehem. We found that baby with his parents camping in the tower. He was wrapped up in priest's underwear, just like we wrap up the lambs so they can be a spotless sacrifice at the Temple. Tell me what you remember."

"Well, that night we were in the fields, watching the sheep. Suddenly, God's angel stood right by us and God's glory blazed everywhere. It was terrifying!

"But the angel reassured us. 'Don't be afraid!' he said. 'I bring you good news of great joy for everyone! A Savior has just been born in David's town, a Savior who is Messiah and Master. And this is how you will recognize him: You will find a baby lying in a manger, wrapped snuggly in strips of cloth!'

"Suddenly, thousands of others joined the angel — the armies of heaven — praising God and saying, 'Glory to God in the highest heaven, and peace on earth to all whom God favors.'

"When the angels went back to heaven, we decided to go to Bethlehem, to see this mind-blowing thing the Lord told us about.'

"We ran to the village and found Mary and Joseph. And there was the baby, lying in the manger. We told everyone we met what the angels had said about this kid, and everyone was blown away!" [Adapted from Luke 8:8-18]

**What do you think it would have been like to see Mary, Joseph, and Jesus that night?**

Emerson was amazed. "Wow Oliver, you're a terrific storyteller. You should write that down!"

"Nah, it would never sell."

Emerson thought differently, but said, "What I remember best is kneeling down next to that manger.

I felt closer to God there than I've ever felt before, even out here under these stars. When I'm out here, I know God is out there somewhere. But kneeling by the manger — it was like God was down here, with us, inside that little kid. You must remember Mary offering for you to hold her baby, and He reached out to you? It was as if He loved you, sheep stink and all. That Priest, he wouldn't let us touch him, but this Baby, He reached right into our hearts."

Oliver looked down. He was getting sleepy now — sleepy enough to crash on cold rocks. He decided to let the beetle go and admitted, "Sometimes, you're right. As much as I'd like to worship in the Temple, I wouldn't change that one night for a lifetime of temple worship. And it didn't end when we left the manger. We told everyone about the angels and the baby. Can you imagine knowing Jesus and not telling others about Him?"

Suddenly, Emerson had a thought. He said it quickly; afraid if he didn't get it out right away it might leave his head forever. "I've one more thought for you, before you give up being a shepherd. That night the angel said, 'Unto you a savior is born.' This baby with God inside didn't come to some pompous priest, or to King Herod or some rabbi. He came to us. Maybe God doesn't see us as unclean. Maybe God our Shepherd loves us in spite of our dirt."

## SO, WHAT SHOULD I DO?

Don't argue with your big brother — he's apt to win.

Don't slap a priest. They might slap back.

Prepare to meet Jesus, because He is coming back, and He loves you sin-stink and all. Jesus wants to wash your sin away, and give you a new life. Turn away from your sin and to Jesus. He will be your Shepherd; He will protect and guide you all the days of your life.

Tell others what Jesus has done for you. Even shepherds know enough to do that.

## WHERE ELSE IS THIS TAUGHT?

### PSALMS 23:1-6

The Lord is my shepherd; I have everything I need. He lets me rest in green meadows; he leads me beside peaceful streams. He renews my strength. He guides me along right paths, bringing honor to his name. Even when I walk through the dark valley of death, I will not be afraid, for you are close beside me. Your rod and your staff protect and comfort me. You prepare a feast for me in the presence of my enemies.

You welcome me as a guest, anointing my head with oil. My cup overflows with blessings. Surely your goodness and unfailing love will pursue me all the days of my life, and I will live in the house of the Lord forever.

**1 SAMUEL 16:7**
The LORD doesn't see things the way you see them. People judge by outward appearance, but the LORD looks at the heart.

**JOHN 10:14-15**
Jesus said: "I am the good shepherd; I know my own sheep, and they know me, just as my Father knows me and I know the Father. So I sacrifice my life for the sheep."

### MORE NOTES FOR THE CURIOUS:

The tower in this story shows up for the first time in the Bible in Genesis 35:19-21. In Hebrew is it is called Mig-dal Ay-dar, but the NLT transliterates it Migdal-eder. From Micah 4:8 and 5:2-5, it seems this was a likely birthplace of Jesus. Micah 4:8 says, "As for you, O watchtower of the flock, O stronghold of the Daughter of Zion, the former dominion will be restored to you; kingship will come to the Daughter of Jerusalem." [NIV] The phrase "watchtower of the flock" is the NLT translation of Mig-dal Ay-dar. The view Jesus was born here has come and gone, but is probably best supported by Alfred Edersheim in The Life and Times of Jesus the Messiah, chapter 6. This isn't a great bed-time reader unless you want to fall asleep, but it is one of the best known and most important references to the life of Christ in print. It's been in publication since 1883. Not a bad run.

Edersheim also talks about the swaddling clothes. Priests would donate their undergarments to the poor after the feast days, and the poor would use them as swaddling clothes. I assume they were more like clean white rags than Fruit of the Loom tighty-whities. Shepherds would raise lambs for the Temple sacrifices, and then wrap them in the free rags to make sure they stayed "without blemish." Since Jerusalem was only four miles away from Bethlehem, and since they used this area to raise temple lambs, it seems likely that Mary and Joseph wrapped up Jesus, our High Priest, in discarded priest's underwear when He was an infant.

## Shepherds

It was an ordinary evening
with ordinary stars
while ordinary shepherds
watched their sheep.

They repeated age-old stories
to keep themselves awake
while listening for sounds
of wolves that creep.

Their eyes popped open wide because
an angel lit the sky.
The shepherds shook with fear.
They couldn't speak.

The messenger from heaven said,
"Messiah has been born!
Fear not, run down the hill
and take a peek."

Those ordinary shepherds blinked,
then clambered down the hill.
They gazed in awe at Jesus
wrapped in white.

What started out as common folks
beneath a common sky
exploded into miracles
of absolute delight.

– Janice Cooley Jones

### STORY 2:

# Don't Name Your Dog Legion

**Scripture Passage:** Philippians 2:6-11

**If you were the richest person in the world, what would you buy?**
...............................................

**Would you give some of your money to help those who had less?**
...............................................

**Wouldn't it be fun to be rich and powerful?**
...............................................

You could buy a new bike and a red sports car, or build a hospital for elderly beetles. You could dig wells to help those without clean water, or buy a belt for everyone who wears saggy pants. Of course, the more money you gave, the less you would have.

This story is about the richest, most powerful person ever - who gave so much away that he became one of the poorest, least powerful, people ever. What is bizarre about it — is that He became poor so He could give His riches to you.

**FROM RICHER TO POORER...**

I HAVE A DOG. His name is Max, but when we don't like him we call him Legion, because his demons are many.

Let's pretend you have a dog. He's a massive, drooling, fun mutt named Legion, and you love him. But, there is something called The Dreaded Dangerous Dog Disease ravaging the country. Only dogs have the disease, but they can pass the disease on to their owners. If a dog with the disease sneezes or rubs his nose on his owner — the owner could get the disease. If a person gets the disease, he or she will die. So, in order to save the people, the authorities decide they have no choice but to kill all the dogs. And, just for fun, let's pretend you somehow know your dog isn't infected, but they are going to kill him, just to be safe.

You try to hide Legion, but he won't stay hidden. You put him in the basement, and he barks and yelps to come back up. You throw rocks at him to get him to run away, but he keeps coming back. You write him a letter and he drools on it. You yell and try to explain things to Legion, but he just licks you.

Finally, you hear some good news. There is a potion that can turn you into a dog. If you drink the potion, you will be able to talk to Legion, and get him to hide so he won't be killed. But there is bad news.

If you drink the potion, you will be a dog forever.

## Would you drink the potion?

No way would I drink it. I like my dog — but not that much. But, for our story, we'll pretend you decide to drink the potion. First, you take off his collar and put it around your neck. Then you take the drink. Unfortunately, as a result, you turn into a small, ugly, Chihuahua. You've gone from being richer - a human, to poorer - a dog.

Immediately you try to talk to your dog.

"Hey Legion, it's me."

"Master? Is that you Master? Mercy, you're ugly. If you were going to become a dog, couldn't you have become a Husky, or a St Bernard, or a Basset Hound? Anything but a Chihuahua!"

"Yeah, I know. It wasn't my choice. I drank this potion to turn me into a dog and — hey you want to go run in the back yard and chase squirrels and birds and eat stinky stuff?"

"Sweet, you are the best master EVER!"

After three hours of chasing squirrels, eating bugs, rolling in dead stuff and smelling beetles to see if they are good to eat (yuck), you both decide to come back inside, take a drink, and drool.

"Wow, this is the best day of my life. Thanks for becoming a dog, Master. By the way, why did you do it? Just to play with me? Just to talk to me?"

"Why did I become a dog? It's hard to remember... To chase birds? No, that's not it. To roll in dead stuff? Nope, but that was fun. And drooling without having to wipe my face, that was my favorite part of the day. Why did I become a dog anyway?"

Knock, knock.

"OH NO! NOW I REMEMBER! LEGION HURRY, RUN AWAY, THEY'RE AT THE DOOR!"

"Who's at the door?"

"The police — I forgot — it's the new law — they're coming to kill you — they're killing all the dogs in the country because of the DDDD — the Dreaded Dangerous Dog Disease. YOU NEED TO RUN NOW!"

KNOCK, KNOCK — OPEN UP, IT'S THE POLICE!

"OK, I'm off. See you later Master! — No. Wait. What about you? You are a dog now too. They will kill you — I won't see you later!"

"Just leave. They have the address of every dog in the country. They know there's a dog in this house. When they see me, you'll be free."

"But what about you?"

"I made my choice when I drank the potion. NOW, GO!"

KNOCK.

**That is the story of Christmas.**

Not that you became a dog to die in the place of your dog. That's just bizarre.

We're like the dog Legion that was going to die. Jesus is like our Master. He came from Heaven to Earth, and became human to save our lives.

Christmas is about God becoming human in order to die in our place.

Paul describes what happened when Jesus left Heaven and came to Earth. He wrote, "Although he [Jesus] was in the form of God and equal with God, he did not take advantage of this equality. 7 Instead, he emptied himself by taking on the form of a servant, by becoming like other humans, by having a human appearance." [Philippians 2:6, GW]

Paul says Jesus was in the form of and equal to God. If you were in the form of a dog — you would be a dog. Jesus was in the form of God — how cool would that be? That means Jesus was around before He made Earth. Maybe He played soccer on the gold streets of Heaven with the angels. Fifteen-hundred years before He was born on earth, He saw the Red Sea split so Moses could walk through. A thousand years before He was born, He watched as David killed Goliath. Jesus had endless knowledge, power, and wealth as God. If He needed anything, all He had to do was to take a chip out of a gold street and buy it! Then Jesus became poor.

**When Jesus came to earth, He was God with human skin on. He still is.**

**But why did Jesus leave heaven and come down here?**

**Didn't He like it up there?**

Jesus left Heaven and came to Earth so He could talk to us, show us how to live, and die in our place. Paul writes that Jesus, "humbled himself by becoming obedient to the point of death, death on a cross." [Philippians 2:8 GW]

God knew we were in danger. We've all sinned, and the result of sin is death. God could have told us to trust Him by writing it in the sky, yelling, throwing rocks at us, or sending us a letter. He had already written the Old Testament for us, but people didn't obey what He wrote.

So, God became a human. The baby at Christmas, Jesus, is God with skin on. He was born like you. He cried, had messy diapers and dirty fingernails. Jesus felt pain, got tired, lonely, and hungry. He was disappointed, and had friends turn against him. He laughed, made jokes, and enjoyed the warm sunshine and a cool breeze. So, He can relate to anything you have experienced. Now we can look at the life of Jesus and know what God is like. We know how we should live when we read about how He lived. There are more words about the life of Jesus than of anyone else in history. Because He was, and is, God.

Jesus became human for us.

But it doesn't end there.

Paul goes on to say, "This is why God has given him [Jesus] an exceptional honor — the name honored above all other names — so that at the name of Jesus everyone in heaven, on earth, and in the world below will kneel and confess that Jesus Christ is Lord to the glory of God the Father. [Philippians 9:9-11 GW]

When Jesus died on the Cross — He was God. He could have come down from the cross whenever He wanted. But He chose stay there — to die in your place. And, because He was innocent, God the Father raised Him from the dead. Now, if you will trust Jesus, He will make certain that you will rise from the dead also.

Jesus was the richest, most powerful person in the world. After all, He is God! But He gave all that up, and put on skin so He could talk to you, die for you, come alive again and offer you forever life. He became poor so you might become rich. Maybe not rich enough to buy a TV game machine as big as a house — but rich because Jesus is rich and will one day give you all the treasures in heaven.

You are familiar with the generosity of our Master, Jesus Christ. Rich as he was, he gave it all away for us — in one stroke he became poor and we became rich. [2 Corinthians 8:8 msg]

## SO, WHAT SHOULD I DO?

Never name your dog Legion. Sometimes pets seem to grow into their names.

Every time you see a manger scene, remember to thank Jesus for becoming poor so you could become rich.

When you get to heaven, don't chip off a hunk of a gold street. It's bad manners.

## WHERE ELSE IS THIS TAUGHT?

### ROMANS 9:5
Christ ... is God, the one who rules over everything and is worthy of eternal praise! Amen.

**ACTS 20:28**
Feed and shepherd God's flock — his (God's) church, purchased with his (God's) own blood. (author's notes)

**ISAIAH 9:6**
For a child is born to us, a son is given to us. The government will rest on his shoulders. And he will be called: Wonderful Counselor, Mighty God, Everlasting Father, Prince of Peace.

**ISAIAH 44:6, REVELATION 1:17**
"This is what the LORD says — Israel's King and Redeemer, the LORD of Heaven's armies: I am the First and the Last; there is no other God" ... When I saw him, I fell at his feet as if I were dead. But he laid his right hand on me and said, "Don't be afraid! I am the First and the Last."

**ISAIAH 40:28, COLOSSIANS 1:16**
The LORD is the everlasting God, the Creator of the ends of the earth... For by him (Jesus) all things were created: things in heaven and on earth... all things were created by him and for him. [NIV] (author's notes)

## MORE NOTES FOR THE CURIOUS:

I really don't have any special notes to put in here, as the above verses explain it all. However, all the other stories have More Notes for the Curious, so this story seemed incomplete without it. If you have any questions about this book or about the Greatest Book of all, our Bible, please shoot me a note at dan@danielcooley.com. Otherwise, let me wish you a MERRY CHRISTMAS, and I hope you enjoy the rest of the book.

# Salvation Baby

How Can I Get to Heaven?

Does it take a village?
Does it take an offering?
Does it take good efforts
like food given to the poor?

Does it take religion?
Does it cost a fortune?
Does it call for auras,
yoga poses on the floor?

You could never do it.
You cannot achieve it.
All it takes is one small sin
to block you from the Gate.

All the good you're doing
will not gain you entrance.
God demands perfection.
Do not fear, it's not too late.

Baby in a manger,
in Bethlehem, a stranger,
came to life on earth
so that for you He could die.

He, the perfect Savior,
is your substitution.
He came down to this earth
to raise you up on High.

JOHN 3:16

– JANICE COOLEY JONES

## STORY 3:

# Don't Mess with Harry

**The Passage:** John 1:1-14

**What do you know about angels?**
..................................................
**Have you ever seen one?**
..................................................
**If not, what do you think they look like?**
..................................................

People have odd ideas about angels. Some people draw them as babies with halos, or beautiful women with wings, or even members of a baseball team. But the Bible tells us what angels are really like.

This story is about Harry the angel, and his Earth-trips.

**LET'S MEET HARRY...**

# How old are you?

That's a question you humans can answer easily — but it's harder for me. You see, I'm an angel, and I'm older than dirt, I mean really — I am older than dirt! Let me explain.

### EARTH-TRIP 1

Jesus made me. We called Him "The Word" [John 1] back then. We didn't call Him Jesus until after He was born on earth. Anyway, one day, thousands of years ago, The Word made me.

One of my earliest memories is watching The Word leaving Heaven. He asked if anyone wanted to go with Him.

"I DO, I DO — PICK ME, PICK ME," I yelled. He picked me, for my first Earth-trip!

We took off together zooming through space. Then we dropped down to this thin, unfinished, dark planet. When we landed, The Word started creating things out of words. He started with, "Let there be light," and in an instant, there were lights. Billions of stars only seconds old appeared — yet He made them billions of years old at the same time. Then He made oceans, trees, dinosaurs, and beetles, just as He made the light. He commanded them into being and there they were — old and full grown — yet young at the same time. After that, He created something differently. He formed people out of mud, and when He breathed into the people, they became alive. That was a day to celebrate! [Job 38:4,7]

### EARTH-TRIP 2

My next trip to earth came thousands of years later, I don't really know how long. Like most angels, I've always liked LOUD music. Sometimes we sing so loud up here in heaven the Temple shakes! [Isaiah 6:3-4] Well, one day we were trying to shake things up again, and had just finished with our sound-check, when The Word got up to speak.

The place became silent.

The Word said, "I'm about to go down to Earth. Yes, I know it's smelly and dirty down there, but I have a way to bring the humans up here. I want to forgive their sins if they will turn from their wicked ways and follow me. Who wants to come with me?"

"I'LL GO, I'LL GO — PICK ME, PICK ME," I yelled. And He picked me — among others.

Now I was SO curious. How would The Word enter the human world? Would He split the skies like He did the Red Sea and then ride down on a flying dinosaur? Would He bring back Noah's Ark just to prove who He is? Would He want us to shine our armor, so He could come with His army of angels to impress the kings of the world?

## How would you come down to earth if you were God?

Then God The Word said, "I will go to Earth by entering the womb of a teenage girl named Mary. In nine months, Mary will give birth to me and name me Jesus [meaning "God Saves"] - the name the humans will call me for time eternal. On the night she gives birth there will be some stinky shepherds watching their flocks on a hill nearby. I need you angels to tell the shepherds, and only the shepherds, who I am."

Then The Word left. I was shocked. I wondered, "What good can a baby do?" It seemed crazy, but nine months later, I left Heaven for Earth, and went to freak out some sleepy shepherds. We tried to make the foundations of Earth shake when we shouted out, "Glory to God in the highest, and on earth peace to men on whom His favor rests!" I wanted to ask the shepherds "Do you understand what we're saying? Do you realize who has come to you? Do you know the gift you've been given? We've been worshiping The Word in the glory of Heaven, now He's put on skin! God came to you!" But they seemed in shock. I told them not to be afraid. The older one bowed in worship or fear, but the younger boy just huddled around a beetle.

## What will happen to this baby? Will the world understand who He is?

About thirty years later, Jesus went out into the desert all alone to spend time with God. Jesus was out of food and water — and then Satan came, tempting him, taunting him. As I was watching, God the Father asked, "Who wants to go help Jesus?" "I'LL GO, I'LL GO — PICK ME, PICK ME," I yelled.

"GO!" He ordered. I raced down to earth as Satan raced away. After giving Jesus food and drink I wondered, "What will happen next?" [Mark 1:12-13] It came too soon.

I was standing at the edge of Heaven, with other angels. Our battle gear was on and our swords were drawn. We were waiting for the order to rescue Jesus. People were telling lies about Him, taunting Him. They tied Him up and whipped him. But this time, the order to rescue Jesus never came. Jesus stayed silent. The Father said nothing. Then I said to myself, "Self," I said, "This can't really be happening! It must be a bad dream!" Because the next thing you know, they crucified Jesus, put His dead body in a cave, and rolled a stone in front of the entrance.

I was horrified and curious. Could the Creator be dead? Could Jesus be just a human, going back to mud? But, I had the best view of what happened next. The Father asked, "Harry, are you ready to shake things up?" "I'LL GO, I'LL GO — PICK ME, PICK ME," I yelled.

"First," He said, "Let me tell you what you get to do."

I raced back down to Earth and went to the Temple. It had a curtain inside to show how far God and man are apart from each other. But this was no ordinary curtain — it was 60 feet high — about as high as 3 houses stacked on top of each other — and 4 inches thick, so that no one could tear it apart. It was so heavy it took 300 priests to hang it up. But I'm not a priest, I'm an angel!

I tore that curtain down the middle from top to bottom. Since God came from Heaven to Earth in the person of Jesus, there is no separation between Heaven and Earth anymore!

Then I smashed down to earth causing an earthquake, and waited for my next orders.

Jesus, alive and ready for action, found me sitting on one of the Temple towers, dangling my legs. "Do me a favor, would you?' He asked, 'I am alive! You know that, I know that — but the humans? They think I'm dead. Would you give those Romans guarding my empty tomb a scare and roll that silly stone away from the cave entrance? They need to see that I AM ALIVE!"

When I showed up, the soldiers guarding the tomb were so shocked they might have messed their clothes. That wasn't something I needed to see, so I ignored them and rolled the stone away for all to see inside. Except for a beetle and a folded up face cloth, it was empty.

I'm told that one day Jesus The Word will ask, "Who wants to go back with me to the Earth? But this time, I'm not going as a baby. I'm returning as the King!" And I'll answer, "I'LL GO, I'LL GO — PICK ME, PICK ME," Meanwhile, we angels are still trying to make the foundations shake again when we sing to Jesus, "Worthy is the Lamb, who was slain, to receive power and wealth and wisdom and strength and honor and glory and praise!" [Revelation 5:12] One day you can join us. Maybe you can sing along and your additional voice is all we will need to shake both Heaven and Earth.

### SO, WHAT SHOULD I DO?

Get ready for Jesus to come back with His angels. Maybe there will be one named Harry.

### WHERE ELSE IS THIS TAUGHT?

### MATTHEW 25:31
When the Son of Man comes in his glory, and all the angels with him, then he will sit upon his glorious throne.

### 2 THESSALONIANS 1:7
God will provide rest for you who are being persecuted and also for us when the Lord Jesus appears from heaven. He will come with his mighty angels.

### REVELATION 22:16
"I, Jesus, have sent my angel to give you this message for the churches. I am both the source of David and the heir to his throne. I am the bright morning star."

### ISAIAH 6:1-4
It was in the year King Uzziah died that I saw the Lord. He was sitting on a lofty throne, and the train of his robe filled the Temple. Attending him were

mighty seraphim, each having six wings. With two wings they covered their faces, with two they covered their feet, and with two they flew. They were calling out to each other, "Holy, holy, holy is the LORD of Heaven's Armies! The whole earth is filled with his glory!" Their voices shook the Temple to its foundations, and the entire building was filled with smoke.

## 1 TIMOTHY 3:16
Without question, this is the great mystery of our faith: Christ was revealed in a human body and vindicated by the Spirit. He was seen by angels and announced to the nations. He was believed in throughout the world and taken to heaven in glory.

### MORE NOTES FOR THE CURIOUS:

Jesus made Angels. Now that seems pretty weird, since Jesus was born just a couple thousand years ago, and angels have been around since before the beginning of the earth. But the Bible teaches that Jesus was around before He was born. In Colossians 1:16 we are told that, "everything, absolutely everything, above and below, visible and invisible, rank after rank after rank of angels — everything got started in him [Jesus] and finds its purpose in him." [msg]

Angels are older than dirt. The angels watched Jesus The Word create our planet, and cheered when He was done. At one point, God asked the man Job… "Where were you when I laid the foundations of the earth … and all the angels shouted for joy?" [Job 38:4,7]

Angels are God's warriors. It's not wise to make your big brother mad. But angels — don't ever make an angel mad! In Psalms 78:49 God uses His angels as an army — and in Revelation Jesus returns to the Earth with an army of angels. One time just one angel killed 185,000 Assyrian soldiers! [Isaiah 37, story in Bizarre Bible Stories 2!]

Angels serve God. Hebrews 1:14 says, "Angels are only servants — spirits sent to care for people who will inherit salvation." God uses them to answer our prayers, protect us, and even to bring us to Heaven. In the book of Exodus, angels freed Israel from Pharaoh by drowning his army in the Red Sea, in the book of Daniel they answered dreams, and in Revelation it says they will come back with Jesus as part of His army to take back planet Earth.

Angels worship God loudly in Heaven. When Isaiah went to Heaven, he interrupted one of their worship services. He said the angels "were calling out to each other, 'Holy, holy, holy is the LORD of Heaven's Armies! The whole earth is filled with his glory!' Their voices shook the Temple to its foundations, and the entire building was filled with smoke." [Isaiah 6:3-4] I wish church was like that on Sundays.

Angels are Curious. 1 Peter 1:12 tells us that angels long to figure out what God is doing. Curiosity can be a good thing.

# Harry

I'm Harry the angel; I'm part of a host.

I work for Jehovah (my reason to boast).

You won't always see me; I
blend in with clouds.

But when I am praising, I get really loud.

I can bring comfort, when
God's children weep.

Or charge with God's army,
and legions defeat.

I'm helping God's children
to fight against sin.

It's my duty, my purpose, to see Jesus win.

One day, if needed, I'll be there for you.

It's my duty, my pleasure; it's just what I do.

– JANICE COOLEY JONES

## STORY 4:

# The Kingmakers

**The Passage:** Matthew 2:1-12

#### Who Am I?

I'm one of these Bible characters you hear about at Christmas time — but I'm not a shepherd or a king or a donkey or a beetle. My ancestors were from a priestly tribe that studied astronomy (the stars), other religions, and science. For hundreds of years my relatives helped pick kings and queens, but we're not royalty. I saw Jesus, but I wasn't there on Christmas Day, and I never lived in Israel. I'm related to Daniel from the Old Testament book of that name, and, like Daniel, I'm a scientist. I have plenty of money, and believe in the God of the Bible.

Who am I?

**LET'S FIND OUT...**

# I'M A MAGI, AND I'm writing to

clear up our story. I hear people sing "We Three Kings" at Christmastime, but no kings came to see Jesus at his birth. King Herod was only about five miles away, but he stayed home. It's us, the Magi who came. Some call us wise men, or scientists, or astrologers, or magicians, but Magi works for me, as it is what we are called in the Bible. Since the Bible doesn't give any of our names, you can call me Memphis. Here is what the Bible does say, in Matthew 2:1.

"After Jesus was born in Bethlehem in Judea, during the time of King Herod, Magi from the east came to Jerusalem 2 and asked, "Where is the one who has been born king of the Jews? We saw his star when it rose and have come to worship him." [NIV2011]

### If you could go back in time, where would you go?

If I could go back in time, I'd go back to around 500 years before Jesus was born. That's when Daniel lived. He was my great, great, great, great, great, well, I'm not sure how many greats go in there — but he was a many-great grandpa of mine. I'll just call him Grandpa. Here's what happened…

Back then, Nebuchadnezzar was king of Babylon. King Neb went to war against Israel, and brought Daniel and some other teenagers back as prisoners. When Daniel and his friends arrived in Babylon, they were sent to Magi School. Daniel was just graduating from that school when King Neb had a dream that totally freaked him out. He woke up all scared and sweaty — so he yelled for his Magi to interpret the dream for him.

"OK King, we will do our best," they said, "just tell us the dream and we will tell you what it means."

But King Neb had forgotten his dream! No matter how hard he tried, he couldn't remember it — and the harder he tried to remember the dream, the more terrified he became. And, the more terrified he became, the harder he tried to remember it. It was a long night. So he told his Magi, "I can't remember it — so you must tell me both the dream I had and what it means."

The Magi answered King Neb, "What? We can't do that! We don't know what you dreamed. We'd have to be some kind of god to know that! No king has ever asked such a thing before, and no one can tell you what you dreamed!"

But King Neb wasn't backing down. He said, "I am serious about this. If you don't tell me what my dream was, and what it means, you will be torn limb from limb, and your houses will be turned into heaps of rubble! But if you tell me what I dreamed and what the dream means, I will give you many wonderful gifts and honors. Just tell me the dream and what it means!" [Daniel 2:5-6]

I wonder what my grandpa thought when he heard that!

> **Have you ever felt like everyone was against you? Without hope? When? Why? Were you really without hope?**

I'd love to go back in time to hear what the Magi said to each other that night. "I don't want to be torn limb from limb — how about we make up a dream and interpret that?"

"But the King will know that's not his dream! He will kill us anyway."

The magi looked at tea leaves, examined the stars, and would have consulted a beetle if they could talk to one — but nothing worked.

Someone asked, "Well do you have any better ideas?"

Grandpa Daniel did.

Grandpa may have been just a teenager in a foreign jail, but he could pray. So pray he did.

That night God answered Grandpa Daniel's prayer, telling him both what the king had dreamt, and what the dream meant. So Grandpa immediately went to King Neb.

When Grandpa Daniel told Neb his dream and its meaning, Neb was blown away! Grandpa become a hero. He was a hero not only to the king, but especially to all the Magi, because he saved them from a gruesome death! After that, some of the Magi became followers of Grandpa's God because they knew only a true God could have told him the dream and saved their lives. But the story doesn't end there.

Later, God sent one of His most powerful angels to Grandpa Daniel, the angel Gabriel. Now that I would love to see! Gabriel told Grandpa a great truth. He said that they wouldn't have to live in Babylon forever, but that Jerusalem, Daniel's home would be rebuilt. And, better than that, He said the Messiah, King Jesus, would come 483 years after someone ordered Jerusalem rebuilt. [Daniel chapter 9]

It wasn't long after Grandpa Daniel died that Jerusalem was rebuilt. Then we Magi started counting down the 483 years until King Jesus would come. We didn't know His name would be Jesus, we just knew Him as the Coming King, Messiah, or Anointed One. During these years, we Magi worked as scientists and king's counselors. When kingdoms were looking for new kings, they would use us to help choose their next leaders. We Magi were the kingmakers. We even helped to choose Queen Esther. In Esther 1:3 we are called the "wise advisers," just another word for Magi.

Then the Bible goes silent about us, until it tells my story in Matthew chapter 2.

> After Jesus was born in Bethlehem in Judea, during the time of King Herod, Magi from the east came to Jerusalem and asked, "Where is the one who has been born king of the Jews? We saw his star when it rose and have come to worship him…"
>
> Then Herod called the Magi secretly and found out from them the exact time the star had appeared. He sent them to Bethlehem and said, "Go and search carefully for the child. As soon as you find him, report to me, so that I too may go and worship him."
>
> After they had heard the king, they went on their way, and the star they had seen when it rose went ahead of them until it stopped over the place where the child was. When they saw the star, they were overjoyed. On coming to the house, they saw the child with his mother

Mary, and they bowed down and worshiped him. Then they opened their treasures and presented him with gifts of gold, frankincense and myrrh. [NIV2011]

When we followed the star to Bethlehem, we weren't coming to help interpret a dream like Grandpa Daniel did for King Neb. We weren't coming to help choose a queen like we did for Esther. We weren't coming to rescue a beetle from a fire. We were the kingmakers, and we were coming to declare and worship the new king, King Jesus.

500 years before Jesus was born, God chose a Magi, Daniel, to tell us when King Jesus would be born. The Magi passed down this information from one generation to the next, all the way down to me. When we saw the strange light in the sky, and knew it had been 483 years since Jerusalem had been rebuilt, we knew it was time to go find and worship our new King.

When we arrived, we expected kings and pastors to be with Jesus. Shoot, we expected King Herod to go with us. But, none of those important people were there. God knew this would happen, and I suppose that is why he told Grandpa Daniel, 500 years before I was born, when to have us show up. He wanted to make sure we Magi, the kingmakers, would be there to declare and worship King Jesus.

## SO WHAT SHOULD I DO?

Worship Jesus.

## WHERE ELSE IS THIS TAUGHT?

### 2 KINGS 17:36
Worship only the LORD, who brought you out of Egypt with great strength and a powerful arm. Bow down to him alone, and offer sacrifices only to him.

### PSALMS 33:18
The LORD watches over those who fear him, those who rely on his unfailing love.

### JEREMIAH 29:33
If you look for me wholeheartedly, you will find me.

### MATTHEW 2:1-2
Jesus was born in Bethlehem in Judea, during the reign of King Herod. About that time some wise men from eastern lands arrived in Jerusalem, asking, "Where is the newborn king of the Jews? We saw his star as it rose, and we have come to worship him."

**MATTHEW 28:8-9**
The women ran quickly from the tomb. They were very frightened but also filled with great joy, and they rushed to give the disciples the angel's message. And as they went, Jesus met them and greeted them. And they ran to him, grasped his feet, and worshiped him.

**PHILIPPIANS 2:10-11**
At the name of Jesus every knee should bow, in heaven and on earth and under the earth, and every tongue confess that Jesus Christ is Lord, to the glory of God the Father.

**HEBREWS 1:6**
And when he brought his firstborn Son into the world, God said, "Let all of God's angels worship him."

**REVELATION 1:5**
Jesus Christ. He is the faithful witness to these things, the first to rise from the dead, and the ruler of all the kings of the world. All glory to him who loves us and has freed us from our sins by shedding his blood for us.

## MORE NOTES FOR THE CURIOUS:

Magi: The word for "Wise Men" or "Magi" can also be translated "scientist, astrologer," or "magician." We don't know much about who these Magi were, but what we do know is pretty cool. We know they were a type of scientist, that they descended from a priestly tribe from a people called the "Medes," and that they studied stars. Some were probably into strange religions, and yet others must have been believers in the True God.

History seems to indicate that after Daniel died, the Magi lived east of Israel in the Parthian Empire. During these years, kings would hire Magi as their counselors. When kingdoms were looking for new kings, they would use the Magi to help choose their next leaders. The Magi were the kingmakers.

483 years: In Daniel chapter nine, the words of Gabriel actually say 69 weeks of years, not 483 years. 69 weeks × 7 years in a week = 483 years. The prophecy also says that this 69 weeks of years "will pass from the time the command is given to rebuild Jerusalem until a ruler — the Anointed One — comes … "After this period … the Anointed One will be killed, appearing to have accomplished nothing …"

So Gabriel not only prophesied about the birth of Jesus the Anointed One, but also about His death. However, the Magi would not have known the exact dates. There were four different decrees to rebuild Jerusalem, so they would only have known the approximate time of his birth, and waited for the sign of the light prophesied by Isaiah. Isaiah 9:2,6-7 "The people who walk in darkness will see a great light. For those who live in a land of deep darkness, a light will shine ... For a child is born to us, a son is given to us. The government will rest on his shoulders. And he will be called: Wonderful Counselor, Mighty God, Everlasting Father, Prince of Peace. His government and its peace will never end. He will rule with fairness and justice from the throne of his ancestor David for all eternity. The passionate commitment of the LORD of Heaven's Armies will make this happen!"

# Wise Men
....................

They plodded along between
high camel humps

with food, clothes, and blankets
rolled up into lumps.

Gold, myrrh, and frankincense
jarred with each bump

as they twisted through mountains
with bushes in clumps.

They lumbered along sitting
high on the backs

of the beasts they were guiding
and keeping on track.

Over-excited, they could
not relax.

They were searching for
Someone and would not turn back.

The light that first startled
them was quite a sight.

It grew bigger and brighter
than comets that night.

It must be a prophecy,
what a delight!

It must be a new king.
Those Wise Men were right.

They stopped at King Herod's
place, causing a stare.

Their questions upset him.
He stifled a glare.

The Jews have a new king?
You must find out WHERE!

In Bethlehem was the child.
Wise Men went there.

Oh, how they honored Him.
Oh how they praised.

And the joy that surrounded
them lasted for days.

It lasted for years and it
won't go away.

Just listen to carolers
singing today!

– Janice Cooley Jones

## STORY 5:

# Strange Sam

**The Passage:** Matthew 2:1-2

**Do you really believe the Christmas Story?**

I mean, do you really believe angels came to earth? That they sang to shepherds? Do you really believe that some people called Magi followed a star to a house in Bethlehem where they found the young child named Jesus?

Sam wondered too.

**LET ME INTRODUCE YOU
TO STRANGE SAM...**

# Sam was very strange.

He was a strangely smart scientist, who had a pet Chihuahua. When he found the dog, the name on his collar was Legion, but he seemed to respond better when Sam called him Master. So that's what Sam called him. He was a weird dog, totally ugly — but exceptionally smart. Master knew how to open doors with his paws, operate the TV remote with his tongue (making it rather slimy), and even seemed to understand what Sam was saying. I tell you all of this, so you will understand what Sam did next.

Sam said to himself, "Self," he said, "I'm going to bring people back from the past to see if the Christmas story is really true — and I'll use Master my dog to do it."

You see, Sam the strangely smart scientist had developed a people-borrowing machine. By that, I mean he could put Master into his machine, send Master into the past, and with a Zap! Master could bring people here, but only for a short time. All someone had to do was to touch the ugly dog, and…

**Zap!**

…here they came.

So, Sam set the people-borrowing machine's date to the time his research showed Jesus had been born, around 0AD. He set the location to Bethlehem.

"Good luck Master, now bring back Christmas!" Sam said as he crammed Master into the machine, locked the door, and hit the green button.

"Yeah, send the ugly dog to do a scientist's work," thought Master.

## ZAP!

When Master arrived in the fields outside Bethlehem, the sheep smell was awful. He did a Chihuahua sneeze, which brought him to the attention of a couple young shepherds a few feet away. One of them said...

"Hey look, Emerson, a dog!"

"A dog? That's no dog, Oliver. It's a rat. KILL IT!" Emerson yelled.

"Is not. It's a dog, look — it's trying to eat my beetle," Oliver said.

"STOP THAT! Crazy Mutt, beetles taste yucky, really sour; however I hear they are crunchy on the outside, soft and chewy on — So Emerson, can I keep him?"

"NO, and don't touch him either. He probably has rabies."

"Come here mangy mutt, come on. That's good. Here, let me pet you."

## ZAP!

Immediately Oliver and Master were back in the people-borrowing machine. Sam let them out and staggered back from the sheep stink. Then he asked …

"So son, what's your name?"

"My name is Oliver, but who are you and where am I? Is that dog magic or something? What happened to Emerson — and the fields — and the sheep — and the smell?"

"Well, the smell you seem to have brought with you. This will be hard to believe, but I'm Sam the Scientist from around 2000 years in your future. I'll send you back to your sheep and smell and Emerson if you just answer one question for me."

"Sure, if I can. Sheep may stink, but that rat dog is disgusting. What's the question?" Oliver asked.

"Have you ever seen angels, or a baby named Jesus born in a manger?"

"Wow! How did you know what happened 2000 years ago? Here's what I remember. One night we — that's my brother Emerson and I — well, we were in the fields outside Bethlehem, watching the sheep.

Suddenly, God's angel stood in front of us with God's glory blazing everywhere. It was terrifying!

"But the angel calmed us down. 'Don't be afraid!' he said. 'I bring you good news of great joy for everyone! A Savior has just been born in David's town, a Savior who is Messiah and Lord. And this is how you will recognize him: You will find a baby lying in a manger, wrapped snuggly in strips of cloth!'

"After we saw the angels, we ran to the village and found Mary and Joseph. And there was the baby, lying in the manger, wrapped in priests' old underwear."

"Underwear? That's weird," said Sam.

"Not really, we keep a lot of old priest's underwear in that tower," answered Oliver.

"Ah, maybe that explains the smell. Okay then, I have an idea to test your story. If your story is true, then Master can come back with an angel!"

Master thought to himself, "WHAT?" he thought, "An angel could kill me!"

"Mercy, sometimes I swear that dog can talk," said Sam.

After Sam stuck Master back in the people-borrowing machine, he adjusted it to an earlier time he guessed the angels may have showed up from talking with Oliver, and he hit the green button again.

**ZAP!**

Sam guessed the time correctly. A bright light immediately blinded Master. He couldn't see, but he could hear Harry the angel, in a voice as loud as an airplane, saying, "Don't be afraid! I bring you good news of great joy for everyone! A Savior has just been born in David's town, a Savior who is Messiah and Lord. And this is how you will recognize him: You will find a baby lying in a manger, wrapped snuggly in strips of cloth!"

"Hey Gabriel, is that a Chihuahua down there?" an angel asked.

"Yes! It's Master, the Chihuahua, which means Sam the Scientist is at it again. We'll need an angel to go set him right," Gabriel replied.

"I'LL GO, I'LL GO — PICK ME, PICK ME," yelled Harry the angel.

"Fine with me, go touch the dog and off you go," Gabriel sighed.

**ZAP!**

Suddenly, Harry stood with Master and Sam and Oliver — with God's glory blazing right through the people-borrowing machine. It was terrifying!

"No need to be afraid" said Harry, "Get up off your knees Sam. I won't hurt you, but I wonder, do you believe in angels now?"

"I do, I do!"

"And you now believe the Christmas Story?"

"Well, I don't want to make an angel mad," Sam admitted. "I've heard how you guys can win a fight. But, I still have one thing that troubles me about the story: how could a star stop over a house? I mean, it would burn up the earth if it even came close, and, if the magi were following a comet or meteorite, it would have been too far away to point out one house. Well, unless it fell on the house, but then everyone would end up dead. Besides, Meteors travel at 160,000 miles an hour, how could it hold still over one house? It's just, well, don't get mad, but it's impossible."

"Well, I could answer this," said Harry. "But let's do it your way — I'll call in a Magi who was there — and no, I won't need Master, or your people-borrowing machine to do it."

### ZOP!

Oh no, this sounded different! Was it a pop or a zap? Oliver checked his pockets. YES, the beetle was still in there, and alive. He didn't like the thought of a beetle popping in his pocket — yuck, but now there was someone else in the room.

"This," said Harry, "is Memphis the Magi. He spent months following that star to Bethlehem.

"Memphis, let me introduce you to these folks. I'm Harry the angel, and this is Sam the scientist who is having trouble believing your part of the Christmas story. Over by the Christmas Tree is Oliver the shepherd with a beetle in his pocket, and Master the dog with exceptional human like qualities. So Memphis, I pulled you here, 2000 years in your future, to explain to Sam about the star you were following to Bethlehem."

"Well, it was a bright light, that's for sure." Memphis began. "Bright light is what the word 'star' means in your Bible. As a scientist, Sam, you should know that. Numbers 24:17, and Isaiah 9:2, said a blazing light would come from the land of Israel to announce the King's birth, so we were looking to the bright lights in the sky around the time King Jesus would be born."

"Do you know what that light was?" asked Sam.

"Well, it couldn't have been a normal star. I suppose God could have made a special star, like how He made a special fish to swallow Jonah. However, I think we followed God's light, His glory, to Bethlehem. We know God gave up His glory when

He became human, nine months before He was born. So maybe, when Mary became pregnant, He put His glory in the sky, and we followed His light to the place where He lived."

"You nailed it!" said Harry. "Jesus, our light, is also our star."

## ZAP!

Here is what happened, "Jesus was born in Bethlehem in Judea, during the reign of King Herod. About that time some wise men from eastern lands arrived in Jerusalem, asking, 'Where is the newborn king of the Jews? We saw his star as it rose, and we have come to worship him.' After this interview the wise men went their way. And the star they had seen in the east guided them to Bethlehem. It went ahead of them and stopped over the place where the child was. When they saw the star, they were filled with joy!" [Matthew 2:1-2, 9-11]

## SO, WHAT SHOULD I DO?

Enjoy the Christmas lights. When you see them remember Jesus gave up His glory when He came to Earth. He did this so He could live a perfect life for you, die for you, rise from the dead, make you a home and come back for you — all because He loves you. Tell Him thanks. About 700 years before Jesus was born, Isaiah was looking forward to His coming. He wrote, "The people who walk in darkness will see a great light. For those who live in a land of deep darkness, a light will shine." [Isaiah 9:2]

## WHERE ELSE IS THIS TAUGHT?

### LEVITICUS 9:24
Fire blazed forth from the LORD's presence

### PSALMS 27:1, 56:13
The LORD is my light and my salvation — so why should I be afraid? The LORD is my fortress, protecting me from danger, so why should I tremble? ... For you have rescued me from death; you have kept my feet from slipping. So now I can walk in your presence, O God, in your life-giving light.

### ISAIAH 9:2,6-7
The people who walk in darkness will see a great light. For those who live in a land of deep darkness, a light will shine... For a child is born to us, a son is given to us. The government will rest on

his shoulders. And he will be called: Wonderful Counselor, Mighty God, Everlasting Father, Prince of Peace. His government and its peace will never end. He will rule with fairness and justice from the throne of his ancestor David for all eternity. The passionate commitment of the LORD of Heaven's Armies will make this happen!

**LUKE 2:8-9**
That night there were shepherds staying in the fields nearby, guarding their flocks of sheep. Suddenly, an angel of the Lord appeared among them, and the radiance of the Lord's glory surrounded them.

**1 PETER 2:9**
God... called you out of the darkness into his wonderful light.

**JOHN 1:3-5**
God created everything through him, and nothing was created except through him. The Word gave life to everything that was created, and his life brought light to everyone. The light shines in the darkness, and the darkness can never extinguish it.

## MORE NOTES FOR THE CURIOUS:

### *Are we certain the Magi didn't follow a real star?*

So far we have counted 70 sextillion stars in our universe. That's 70,000,000,000,000,000,000,000, a seven with twenty-two zeros. Could one of them have come close and led the wise men to the house? That's not likely, because if we were any closer to our closest star, the Sun, we would burn up. If our Sun or another star hung over one house, it would burn up the planet. So, no.

### *Could the Magi have followed a meteorite or comet?*

It would have been difficult to see and follow in the daytime. Not only that, but meteors travel at around 160,000 miles an hour, comets can travel over 200 miles in a second. Do you think you could follow a comet on a camel? So, nothing we know of seems to fit what Matthew wrote — that a light was their guide day and night, and that light stood still over one house — except that God led them supernaturally — maybe with His own glory.

### *What other Bible stories show God as light?*

The first thing God created was light in Genesis 1. The Bible often compares God to a fire. God's glory is like a fire, He came to Moses as a fire in the burning bush, He led the Israelites out of Egypt in a pillar of fire [Exodus 13–14], and Jesus will return as an all-consuming fire [Isaiah 33:14]. Jesus is our star.

### *Could Jesus have been the Chanukah light?*

Maybe you have some friends who keep the feast of Chanukah, that comes around the time of Christmas. In Jesus' time, there was an oil candle in the Temple which represented the glory of God. It was put out when a wicked ruler desecrated the temple. However, on the 25th of Kislev (our December) in 165BC the temple was rededicated, and the candle, representing the glory of God, was relit. That's why Chanukah is called "the festival of lights."

When Jesus lived, he kept Chanukah because Chanukah is about Him. Jesus said, "I am the light of the world. If you follow me, you won't have to walk in darkness, because you will have the light that leads to life." [John 8:12]

God made certain a light was in the Temple to illustrate His Glory. He knew He would use His light to bring the Wise Men to Bethlehem, and He knew we would celebrate with lights 2000 years later at Christmas to remember the birth of Christ. He truly is the Light of the World.

# Light

One night the sky was filled with shine,
dispersing all the other lights.
It was a new, distinct design
that aimed at earth with all its might.

Some folks would say it was a star,
for nothing else could be so bright.
But could it travel down so far?
Three watchful Magi got it right.

A sign from heaven was the source.
It was not formed by things finite.
It took a miracle, of course!
It took our God to get it right.

It took our King to note the time
and cause the heavens to ignite.
His precious son appeared, sublime;
Bethlehem town, unlikely site.

He is the Way, the Prince of Peace.
He our souls yearnings can incite.
We bow to Him, our sins release.
This Babe's our friend. What a delight!

– JANICE COOLEY JONES

## ABOUT AUTHOR DAN COOLEY AND POET JANICE COOLEY JONES

Dan and his family love Anchor Point Church, life, reading, writing, camping and shooting, large dogs, *The Princess Bride, Napoleon Dynamite,* green chili, hot weather, Mexican food — and chocolate.

Dan and JoLynn have four children and four grandchildren — Oliver, Emerson who loves playing with bugs, Harrison the angel, and Memphis who is as smart as a magi.

Janice Cooley Jones, the poem writer, is Dan's older sister. Janice and her husband live in the foothills of California. They enjoy days with their granddaughter, trips to the ocean, swimming in the pool at their mobile home park, reading, and writing. Janice enjoys being in a writer's group and teaching Sunday School at Calvary Bible Church. She used to enjoy water skiing. But that was then, and this is now.

Janice has been published in Highlights Magazine, Time of Singing, Bible Advocate, and other adult and children's publications.

Follow Dan: **www.danielcooley.com**

Follow Janice: **www.janicecooleyjones.com**

# If you liked
# Bizarre Christmas Bible Stories,
# check out:

## Bizarre Bible Stories
by Dan Cooley

Flying Pigs, Walking Bones, and 24 Other Things That Really Happened!

**FOR AGES 7 AND UP**

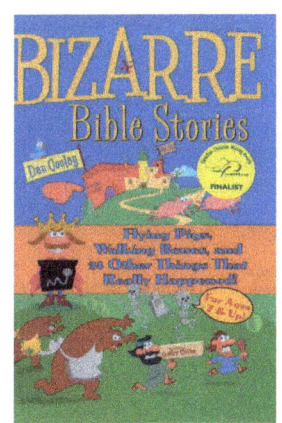

## Bizarre Bible Stories 2
by Dan Cooley

A King in a Suitcase, An Escape Through a Toilet, and 23 Other Things That Really Happened!

**FOR AGES 10 AND UP**

www.ingramcontent.com/pod-product-compliance
Lightning Source LLC
Chambersburg PA
CBHW062043290426
44109CB00026B/2710